Dumfries

Through the Lens
Glimpses of old
New Galloway

Compiled and edited by
Ronald Russell

Dumfries and Galloway
Libraries, Information and Archives
with the Royal Burgh of New Galloway
and Kells Community Council
2002

Designed by Dumfries and Galloway Libraries, Information
and Archives. Set and printed by Solway Offset Services,
Catherinefield Industrial Estate, Dumfries for the publisher.

Dumfries and Galloway Libraries, Information and Archives
Central Support Unit, Catherine Street
Dumfries DG1 1JB
Tel: 01387 252070   Fax: 01387 260294
www.dumgal.gov.uk/lia

ISBN 0 946280 56 8
New Galloway is number 22 in the
Dumfries and Galloway: Through the Lens series.
For a full list of our publications contact us at the above address.

ACKNOWLEDGEMENTS

Mr & Mrs E Muir, Mrs L Thomson, Mr L Paterson,
Dr Innes Macleod, Dr David Devereux, Mrs J
Adair, Mrs A McGill, Kells School, Mr J McPhee,
Mr G Norris, Miss J Murray, Dr Shelagh Neil, the
Lawrie family and all those who kindly loaned
photographs for this publication.

INTRODUCTION

New Galloway, or Newtoun (New Town) of Galloway as it was often known in early days, was established on its present site in the parish of Kells in 1630. It was the brainchild of Sir John Gordon, who obtained a royal charter authorising its creation. Sir John, who was the sixth Laird of Kenmure, was ennobled as the first Viscount Kenmure in 1633, but died in the following year.

Any hopes that its founder may have had for the development of his royal burgh into a rival to Kirkcudbright were frustrated by his own untimely death and the early deaths of the second and third viscounts and also by the Civil War in which the fourth viscount supported the losing side. In the various tax rolls New Galloway held place as the poorest of the royal burghs. In 1664 it paid a mere £11.2s 6d and in 1670 it was entered on the tax roll for one shilling. In 1705 it was granted £40 'in consideration of the low and decayed condition of the burgh'.

Although its population never rose much above 400, New Galloway was important locally for its three annual fairs, its weekly market, and especially as a centre for the cattle droving trade. The fields by Carson's Knowe became a collecting place for the black cattle from the surrounding area and served also as a half-way house between Wigtown and Dumfries. In 1778 the Belfast Almanack quoted the New Galloway Fair as one of the principal sales in the south of Scotland.

Robert Heron, writing in 1792, described the situation of New Galloway as *one of the most delightful that fancy can conceive to exist in a wild country*. He commented on the usefulness of its weekly market, the convenience of its post office, its meal mill and its school, but he was less enthusiastic about the state of its roads and the limitations of its inns. Heron's description of the burgh itself, however, still holds good:

The little gardens of the citizens lie close behind their houses, above and below the town: they are divided by hedges; and trees rise around, or here and there among them: the spire of the court-house is a distinguished object in the groupe: And when the smoke rises from the little chimnies; and the whole is viewed either from an elevation above, or from below; no assemblage of objects can be conceived more pleasing to the eye, and the imagination.

An official report on New Galloway in 1831 referred to it as *a poor place, without Trade or Manufactures, and has no appearance of increasing*. The 1841 census, however, showed that there were twelve shoemakers, including their apprentices, in the burgh, and, among others, seven tailors, six dressmakers, eight masons, three blacksmiths, three schoolmasters, one schoolmistress, a surgeon and a straw-hat maker. There were also forty-six agricultural labourers, seventeen female servants and five male servants. With the opening of the railway from Castle Douglas to Stranraer in 1861, a small tourist trade began to develop, even though New Galloway station was a good five miles from the burgh. A few large houses were built and some of the smaller ones were enlarged. But the resident population hardly increased. Here the Valuation Rolls may provide a clue. Whereas in the seventeenth century the parishes of Kells and Dalry were held by fourteen and seventeen proprietors respectively, in 1874 Kells was shared by only thirteen proprietors while Dalry had dramatically increased to eighty. For New Galloway a situation that provided no incentive to would-be entrepreneurs was not conducive to growth or prosperity.

In 1951 the population of New Galloway was a meagre 305, compared with 462 in 1861 – the highest figure recorded since the beginning of the national census. Since then, improvements in housing and the development of road transport have helped the local economy to some extent and the beauty of its situation has drawn people from elsewhere in Scotland, and from south of the Border, to make their homes in the burgh. Although much has been lost, including several shops and trades, there is now a new Medical Centre, a Community Arts Centre in an advanced planning stage, and plenty of accommodation available for tourists who are attracted by the challenging golf course, the leisure and sporting facilities available on Loch Ken and the proximity of the Galloway Forest Park. In New Galloway itself there are signs of a new vitality, an awareness that this is a very special place with a unique history and a charm entirely of its own.

NEW GALLOWAY

New Galloway in 1801, from a copper engraving by James Fittler after a painting by John Claude Nattes. Nattes was a well-known artist in his day and exhibited frequently in the Royal Academy. This print was published in his book *Scotia Depicta*. The text describes New Galloway as *a remarkably healthy place* with about 300 inhabitants. Note the crescent of buildings behind the right hand-side of the High Street that does not appear in any other illustration of the Burgh and of which no trace remains.

NEW GALLOWAY FROM THE AYR ROAD
The building on the left with the small spire and tall chimneys is partly occupied by the local branch of the Clydesdale Bank; behind it is Mrs Sinclair's stackyard. It is just possible to discern Kenmure Castle through a gap in the trees. The High Street, busy with people, is in the centre with the roof of Meadowcroft visible on the left and the chimneys of Greenhead on the right. The photograph dates from before the 1914 War.

HIGH STREET, NEW GALLOWAY

New Galloway had one of the earliest post offices in the south of Scotland. It travelled up and down the High Street: in this view, when it also acted as
as agency for Raleigh bicycles, it occupied the premises that later became a dress shop called *Pillar Box*. The post office then spent a short time lower
down the street in premises later known as *Paraphernalia* before moving to its present home. On the left is Miss McJanet's sweetshop that also sold
home-made lemonade. Robert Cowan's grocery store occupied a large three-storey house built about 1860. It was the home of a sea captain, who
lined the walls and ceilings with splendid timber panels from his vessel broken up at Palnackie. It is now Kitty's Tearoom.

NEW GALLOWAY, HIGH STREET

This is one of several postcards issued by Mr Mitchell, the postmaster. It was printed in Saxony and colour tinted. The first house on the right was the Mill House, which retains its name today, and next to it is one of the many premises that at one time or another housed the post office. Coal is being delivered further up the street. By the number of carefully posed children in the picture, it must have been taken on a school holiday or perhaps on a weekend. There are fifteen listed buildings of special regional and local interest in New Galloway, nine of them in the High Street itself including the Town Hall.

WEST PORT, NEW GALLOWAY

West Port was part of the Old Edinburgh Road that followed much of the line of the pilgrim route from Whithorn to Edinburgh. It crosses the High Street by the Town Hall and continues downhill towards Carson's Knowe, in years past site of the three annual fairs and the weekly markets. The continuation is signposted Duke Street instead of East Port, although who the duke was no one knows. It is said that the name was a signwriter's error, following local pronunciation, for Duck Street – which makes more sense as ducks once abounded thereabouts. The Town Hall clock was installed in 1872. It was made by Messrs Gillet & Brand, of Croydon, for £120 and was set in motion by Mrs Maxwell of Glenlee, a generous contributor. Its predecessor, now in the Stewartry Museum, was said to be *in utterly worthless condition as a timekeeper.*

SUNNYSIDE, ON WYLIE'S BRAE
Sunnyside is the name of the terrace of four houses nearest the camera. At the foot of the brae is Douglas Place; the roofless cottage was replaced by the earliest Council houses. Wylie's Brae, known as Morningside in the early 19th century, connects the High Street with Carson's Knowe and would have been very busy during the three annual Fairs and the weekly market with men going to and from the inns and the seven alehouses that appeared at appropriate times in the Burgh. Carson's Knowe was also very busy in droving days when New Galloway became famous as the half-way house between Wigtownshire and Dumfries and when cattle from the Stewartry also collected there.

EPISCOPAL CHURCH OF ST MARGARET OF SCOTLAND
A London architect, W H Harrison, drew up the plans and the builders were R Johnstone and W Harley of New Galloway. Funds for the building were raised locally and the cost came to £512.12s, which was almost exactly the amount that was subscribed. This view shows the church before the chancel was added in 1908. This was commissioned by Mr A F M Spalding, of The Holm, Balmaclellan, as a memorial to his sister, the Hon Mrs John Grey. The lych gate was erected in memory of Mr Spalding who died in 1911.

KELLS CHURCH

Ainslie's map of 1797 shows both church and manse in the same positions as they are now, but the present church by the New Galloway architect and builder William McCandlish dates from 1822. The original Kells Church was about a mile away close to Achie Farm. After the new church was built, the old one was used for occasional preaching only until the roof fell in and the walls were pulled down to provide material for dykes and farm buildings. Several gravestones from the old church were carried across to the present churchyard. The first manse, close to the present site, was built in 1742-3; in 1776 it was described as *a low, one-storied thatched house* quite unsuitable for a minister with a family. The oldest part of the present manse dates from 1806.

GRAVESTONE, KELLS CHURCHYARD

Kells churchyard holds a splendid collection of 18th century gravestones. This well-known example was erected by Captain John Gordon of Kenmure in memory of John Murray, a gamekeeper for 46 years, who died in 1777, aged 61. It shows his gun, powder-flask, fishing-rod, dog and a gamebird. The lines on the reverse of the stone were composed by the minister, Mr Gillespie. Miss Ruth and Miss Elspeth Macleod act as supporters in this photograph.

It was Murray who caught the famous 72lb pike in Loch Ken. The inscription reads as follows:

Ah, John, what changes since I saw thee last; Thy fishing and thy shooting days are past. Bagpipes and hautboys thou canst sound no more; Thy nods, grimaces, winks, and pranks are o'er. Thy harmless, queerish, incoherent talk, Thy wild vivacity, and trudging walk Will soon be quite forgot. Thy joys on earth – A snuff, a glass, riddles and noisy mirth – Are vanished all. Yet blest, I hope, thou art, For in thy station, weel thou play'dst thy part.

PROCLAMATION OF KING GEORGE V

This took place outside the Town Hall, May 9, 1910. Most of the present building dates from 1875-6 when the Hall was rebuilt and enlarged. The timbers of an older, narrower spire are encased in the present spire. Two bells inside the spire were originally cast in Edinburgh in 1711, which helps to date the building of the earlier Town Hall. The main hall is dominated by a splendid oil painting of Kenmure Castle and the Town Park by James Faed, jun., which he presented to the Burgh after it was exhibited at the Royal Academy. It was unveiled by Mrs Faed and Mrs Maitland Gordon on August 31, 1893.

NEW GALLOWAY GALA
The Creetown Silver Band passing the Cross Keys Hotel during the 1951 Gala celebrations. The oldest part of the Cross Keys dates from the late 18th century and the hotel itself was much enlarged shortly before the first World War. In Maxwell's *Guide to the Stewartry*, 1902, the then proprietor, William Milligan, offered excellent stabling and horses and carriages for hire on the shortest notice. Like the Kenmure Arms, the Cross Keys provided transport twice daily to New Galloway Railway Station. Mr Milligan described his hotel as *one of the most comfortable Houses for Tourists and Commercial Gentlemen.*

NEW GALLOWAY SMITHY

The Smithy functioned as such until 1940. It was then bought by James Holmes, a plumber, for £8. Since then, after several changes of ownership, it has been extended and converted into an attractive and popular café and gift shop. The smithy itself occupied the area adjacent to the burn and there used to be a mill where the gift shop extension now stands. The old Mill House faced the High Street and the house next to it was one of the many High Street sites once accommodating the post office, where Miss Laurie was postmistress for many years.

13

KENMURE CASTLE
This photograph shows a water-colour of Kenmure Castle and Loch Ken, by James Faed, jun. It was published in *Galloway Water-Colours* in 1919. James Faed was a member of the famous Faed family of artists, son of James and nephew of John and Tom. He painted in both oils and watercolours and first exhibited at the Royal Scottish Academy in 1876. Six of his paintings, including the one he presented to New Galloway, were exhibited at the Royal Academy in London. James spent the last years of his life at *The Bungalow* on the outskirts of New Galloway. The house named *Cairnraws* now occupies that site. Despite illness in those years, he painted almost to the end of his life, using his mouth when his hands would not work.

KENMURE CASTLE, 1909
At that time the castle stood amidst landscaped gardens, with greenhouses, archery butts, tennis courts and walled garden. The oldest part of the present structure dates from the late 16th century when it was rebuilt following its destruction by the Regent Moray as punishment for Sir John Gordon's support of Queen Mary. It was besieged by Cromwell's troops in 1650 and forced to surrender. William, sixth Viscount Kenmure, took part in the 1715 Jacobite rebellion and was executed for high treason. The title was then forfeited until 1822 when it was restored to his descendant John who became the seventh viscount. John held tenure of the estate for 68 years and restored the castle, which was in ruinous condition with the estate deeply in debt when he took it over. In 1840 he was succeeded by his nephew Adam, who had served at Trafalgar, but on Adam's death in 1872 the title became dormant.

KENMURE CASTLE, AERIAL VIEW

An aerial view of Kenmure Castle, shortly after the roof was removed in the late 1950s. On the death in 1872 of Adam, the 8th and last Viscount Kenmure, his sister Louisa Bellamy-Gordon inherited the estates and oversaw several alterations and additions to the building. When she died in 1886 her daughter, also Louisa, let the castle, preferring to live in Overton. The castle continued to be let until Louisa's grandson John Maitland Gordon sold it in 1935. General MacEwan, retired, at that time officer commanding the local Home Guard, rented it during the war. In 1951 it was converted into a hotel by Mr Stanley Dobson, son of the artist Henry Dobson, and Mr Hugh Ormond-Sparks, a tenor vocalist. The project failed and in the following years a demolition firm stripped out the interior and a subsequent owner gave up the idea of restoring the castle and had the roof removed in the hope of avoiding taxation. The ruinous building was bought in the early 1960s by Mr Graeme Gordon, a descendant of the Gordons of Lochinvar.

KEN BRIDGE
This handsome five-arch granite bridge was designed by Sir John Rennie and built in 1821-2. It is 340 ft long with a carriageway of 18ft 3in. An earlier three-arch bridge downstream, also by Rennie and completed in 1811, was destroyed by floods. Two previous attempts to bridge the Ken at this point in the later years of the 18th century had met a similar fate. Before the changes effected by the Galloway Hydro-Electric Scheme, silt carried downriver and deposited on low-lying land by floods greatly enriched the fields in the flood plain. The Ken Bridge Hotel stands at the West end of the bridge.

KEN BRIDGE HOTEL
The hotel on the Ayr-Castle Douglas road beside Rennie's Ken Bridge began life as a small coaching inn dating from about 1796. It used to be called The Spalding Arms after the owner of the land on which it was built. The hotel has been extended around the original building and now has ten bedrooms and a comfortable restaurant. Guests can enjoy free fishing in the adjacent River Ken.

GLENLEE POWER STATION TRANSFORMER
A Pickford's traction engine hauling the transformer for Glenlee Power Station. Glenlee was one of the five original power stations on the Galloway Hydro-Electric Scheme and began supplying power to the National Grid in March 1935. The Galloway scheme on completion was the largest integrated hydro-electric system in Britain.

GLENLEE POWER STATION TRANSFORMER

The transformer for Glenlee trundles down New Galloway High Street. There was much opposition, especially from those with fishing rights, to the Hydro-Electric Scheme and the promoters went to great trouble and expense to provide fish passes, ladders and resting pools. In a speech in 1938 at the unveiling of a memorial to the engineer William McLellan, Lord Meston, chairman of the company, spoke as follows: *In the execution of this work, hands have had to be laid upon the beauties of the country. Power houses, dams, aqueducts, surge towers now dot the valley and it will take time for them to merge into the hues and contours of the landscape, but in at least a partial compensation a whole series of new lochs have been created which will grow in attractiveness as nature takes them into its care.*

GLENLEE POWER STATION, 1934

Note the pipe bringing water from Clatteringshaws Loch, via a 3.5 mile tunnel, completed in October 1933. The tunnel, excavated through hard rock, was the most costly and difficult undertaking in the entire Galloway Hydro-Electric scheme. Five hundred men were employed on its construction; many were injured and two were killed. New Galloway was permitted to draw off water from the tunnel to augment its existing supply, which often proved inadequate in dry weather, at the rate of six pence per thousand gallons.

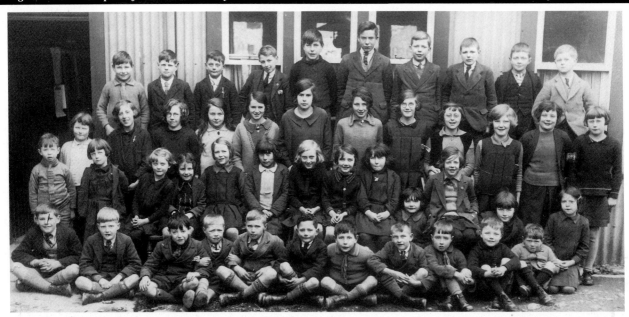

KELLS SCHOOL, ABOUT 1929

From left to right: back row: J Latimer, C Jardine, W Martin, J D Garmory, J A Latimer, W Plunket, J Webster, R M Garmory, A McKnight, D Wilson. Second row: J McQueen, J Stewart, M Campbell, I McKnight, J Fraser, M J H Wilson, S Walker, M J McK Robb, A Milligan, I McGill, S Martin, A M Robb. Third row: R Muir, M Stewart, P Bell, L McWilliam, M Rogerson, J M Douglas, M Carson, V McMinn, H Stewart, J Dargavel, J Robb, M Stewaryt, J Chesney. Front row: J Paterson, R McGill, C Robertson, R Johnstone, T Robb, J Martin, W Latimer, T McIntyre, W Walker, E McNaught, H Martin. The building now known as the *Old School* dates from the late 19th century, when the schoolmaster was James McAndrew, a well-known botanist and editor of *The Flora of Kirkcudbrightshire*. The first schoolmaster named in the records was Alexander Buchanan, in 1743. In 1790 there were 36 scholars, who studied English, writing and arithmetic, with a few also learning Latin. A particularly celebrated schoolmaster was John Muir, who held the post for 44 years until he died in 1864. He was also Collector of Rates, registrar, provost of New Galloway in 1854, and for many years the local postmaster. A school at Polharrow was founded in 1842 and there was also a school at Mossdale from about 1870-1950. The Old School building is being converted into the Glenkens Community and Arts Centre.

KELLS SCHOOL

The Millennium Photograph. The present school building was opened in 1964. There are 48 pupils and 4 teachers. This excellent primary school has a high reputation for music and its choir has won several trophies. Altogether the school makes a valuable contribution to the life of New Galloway and is strongly supported by parents and by the community at large.

NEW GALLOWAY CAMERON HIGHLANDERS AT THE FRONT, 1915
Back row, left to right: Private James Black (wounded), Lance-Corporal Adam Byers, Private Thomas Templeton (wounded), Lance-Corporal John N Rogerson (wounded and missing). Front row, left to right: Private Robert Garmory (wounded), Private John Little, Private William T Stewart (wounded), Lance-Corporal W McGeoch. Private Garmory was the son of ex-Provost Garmory of the Mulloch; Private Stewart's mother was a former owner of the Cross Keys; Private Templeton's father was shepherd at Stranfasket; Lance-Corporal Rogerson (who was thought to have been taken prisoner) used to work for Mr R Cowan in the High Street; Lance-Corporal McGeoch's aunt, Mrs W Murray, lived in West Port. Private Geddes, son of the late George Geddes, mineral agents at New Galloway Station, was wounded and in hospital, as was Private Black, son of Mr Black, gardener at Ardlaggan.

TERRITORIAL ARMY

New Galloway members of the Territorial Army at the back of the Kenmure Arms. The object on the left is a thermometer, such as were commonly seen outside garages in the 1930s. The photograph dates from about 1935.

NEW GALLOWAY FIRE CREW, 1955
They are shown here with their Coventry Climax Major Pump. From left to right: John McCubbin, Jack Macdonald, Alec McCubbing, Davey McCall, Robert Murray, John McQueen. In the early days of the Fire Crew some 15 years before this photograph, a second-hand Klaxon horn was bought for four shillings for *Fire Warning* and equipment included a stirrup pump and a torch. Prior to purchase of their uniforms, the crew's only protective clothing were rubber boots, costing twelve shillings eleven pence a pair. In 1941 a 22hp Austin van was purchased for about £20.

NEW GALLOWAY FIRE CREW
Here we see the Fire Crew on a training exercise with their new van. New Galloway was part of the South Western Fire Area. Water would be pumped from Loch Ken for the purpose of the exercise.

NEW GALLOWAY FIRE CREW, 2001
Back row, from left to right: Frank McGhie, Ian Fergusson, Murray Walker, John McGaw, Michael Lawrie, Peter McDonald. Front row: Bernard Jones, Eddie Millar, Jimmy McKenna, Peter Hamilton. New Galloway has a fine new Fire Station housing a Renault/Dodge Compact Fire Engine, first registered in 1987 and carrying 400 litres of water.

CROQUET ON THE LAWN, THE COTTAGE, NEW GALLOWAY
The house, at the entrance to the Burgh from the Ken Bridge, was built in 1897-8 on a field belonging to Bankend Farm. There was not a single tree or bush on the ground at that time. It was for many years the home of the Courtenay family who were largely concerned with the building and maintenance of St Margaret's Church. In 1935, after many years service on the Council, Mr J A Courtenay was elected Provost. He continued in office until his death in 1943.

NEW GALLOWAY GOLF COURSE, AUGUST 16, 1928

D McCulloch (Troon) and J McDowall (Turnberry) on the second tee. The formation of a Golf Club was first proposed at a meeting in January 1902, when Mr Maitland Gordon offered the use of the Town Park and the adjoining *whinnie field* for a nine-hole course. George Baillie from Musselburgh, a well-known course designer, was commissioned to lay out the course. He wrote, *Few nine-hole courses not lying along the coast will compare with the one at present being laid out close to the town of New Galloway. From start to finish nature has provided both teeing grounds and putting greens, and the rabbit has during many years – perhaps centuries – so nibbled and patted the intervening turf that it resembles that of a seaside links rather than an inland one.*

FISHING IN THE RIVER DEE AT MOSSDALE
The Dee (or Black Water of Dee) forms much of the southern boundary of the parish of Kells. Its waters supply Clatteringshaws Loch, which was created as part of the Galloway Hydro-Electric Scheme, and flow in and out of Loch Ken before entering the Solway Firth at Kirkcudbright Bay. The Dee used to be well regarded as a salmon river; grilse, sea trout, river trout, pike and perch could also be fished, according to Maxwell's *Guide*, 1902. Whether the elegantly posed lady was successful is not known.

31

NEW GALLOWAY GALA WEEK
As its contribution to the Festival of Britain celebrations in July, 1951, New Galloway held a Gala Week. Among the features was a mannequin parade in the Town Hall, organised by the Ladies' Committee convened by Mrs S A Douglas. Young ladies from New Galloway and Castle Douglas took part. Here is part of the display of period dresses loaned by people in the district. The local newspaper commented: *The large audience gave the mannequins a very warm reception, and not the least interested section was the considerable number of men present who appeared to enjoy themselves thoroughly.*

FANCY DRESS PARADE, NEW GALLOWAY GALA WEEK
A children's Fancy Dress parade was held in the Park as part of the 1951 Gala Week celebrations. This prizewinners included Hugh McCreadie, Norman Maxwell, Dunetta Hyslop, Carol McDonald and Beryl and Angela Geddie from Pitlochry. The celebrations included an open-air service with the Creetown Prize Silver Band, a handicraft exhibition, a football match, mounted sports and a parade through the be-flagged town.

NEW GALLOWAY STATION
The station was on the east side of the bridge. It had two platforms and a passing loop; the main building was on the up platform and behind it were three sidings and a small goods shed. The line from Castle Douglas to Stranraer was opened in 1861 and closed under the Beeching dispositions in 1965. There were three, sometimes four, stopping trains a day in each direction and a daily goods train. In the early days a horse-drawn carriage service organised by the Kenmure Arms and the Cross Keys took passengers to and from New Galloway, the journey taking about 45 minutes.

NEW GALLOWAY STATION
The freight train from Stranraer awaits the oncoming passenger train before it can proceed onto the single line. Two of the surviving major engineering features on the line are close to the station: the impressive Ken viaduct, with three bowstring girder spans with masonry piers and abutments, described by the Dumfries Courier as *not only a stupendous but a most elegant erection*, and the four-arch viaduct across the Dee by Loch Stroan.

NEW GALLOWAY STATION
Double-header from Stranraer approaching New Galloway Station. The Portpatrick Railway became a vital link in the Irish traffic with through carriages from London and Glasgow to Stranraer. The evening train from Stranraer was known as the Paddy and, as David Smith says in *The Little Railways of Scotland, in many a lonely cottage they listened for its passing in the dead of night.* On June 12, 1965, the last Paddy, the night sleeper to London, passed through New Galloway Station and the familiar sounds were to be heard no more.

Dalry. Knocknalling House

KNOCKNALLING

John Kennedy, whose story is told in Samuel Smiles' *Lives of the Engineers*, was born at Knocknalling in 1769. His grandfather had been a Bailie and a shopkeeper in New Galloway and saved enough money to buy the Knocknalling estate from another branch of the Kennedy family. At the age of 15 John left home to become an apprentice to a cotton spinner near Manchester. In 1794 he went into business in Manchester as a machine maker in partnership with James McConel, also from the Glenkens. They built three mills in Manchester and soon became the largest cotton spinners in the UK. Kennedy became a director of the Liverpool and Manchester Railway and numbered James Watt and George Stephenson among his friends. On the death of his elder brother he became Laird of Knockalling, rebuilding the house in 1840. He added considerably to the estates, founded a school at Polharrow, continued to create inventions including a spinning wheel for elderly ladies, and was esteemed for his kindness and generosity. He died at his Manchester home, Ardwick Hall, in 1865. Knocknalling is in Kells parish - not, as the postcard says, in Dalry.

37

OVERTON

This house was once part of the Kenmure estate. Louisa Maitland-Gordon, widow of the Revd James Maitland and niece of the 8th Viscount Kenmure, had no desire to live in Kenmure Castle and moved to Overton on the far side of New Galloway. Thereafter no member of the family lived in the castle. Overton dates from about 1818 and was probably built by William McCandlish. There is a contemporary doocot in the grounds. The house was sold in 1942. It became a family home, and then for a time an Old People's Home. It is now in private ownership and is being restored.

GARROCH

Garroch and its neighbour Glenlee are both shown on Timothy Pont's 1595 survey. The first *Manor House* was what is now known as Old Garroch, built about 1700. The house in the photograph dates from 1843 and was built by William Grierson-Yourston. For many years it was known as Ballingear but reverted to its original name in the 1890s when it was owned by Jasper Young, a business man in Singapore. He made major alterations to the house, digging away the land on two sides so that the basement rooms were opened to daylight. His son Arthur modernised the house in 1919, but in 1932 it was badly damaged by fire although most of the contents were rescued. The insurance was sufficient to have the house rebuilt. On Arthur's death in 1951, a year after the death of his wife Rose, his inheritors soon became aware that they could not afford to run and maintain such a large residence. They had it demolished and extended the bothy and stable block to provide a home.

J PATERSON, BUTCHER

John Paterson, butcher of New Galloway, delivering meat in Main Street, Dalry. Mr Paterson joined the Council in 1909, becoming Provost in 1945 and continuing in office until his death in 1960, an outstanding record of service. The butcher's shop in New Galloway High Street traded for nearly 140 years but closed in 2001. At one time there were three slaughterhouses in the Burgh.

THE TOWN COUNCIL, 1975

From left to right: Bob Wood, Jimmy Douglas, John McCubbin, Provost Jack Paterson, Alec Coulthart, Bettie Lewin, John Bertram, Ewart Muir. This was the last Town Council of the Royal Burgh. Henceforth it was the Community Council that was to be responsible for local matters. The provost's chain, the purchase of which was funded by the proceeds of dances in the Town Hall, was removed to Kirkcudbright and is permitted to return to New Galloway only on major occasions. The chairman of the Community Council is still known as the provost.

THE ONE THAT GOT AWAY

Was it really as big as that? Davie Murray, John Turner and Bob Dargavel look and listen as Gordon Milligan tells his fishing tale. They are sitting outside the Co-op store, now Kitty's Tearoom, in 1955.

GRILSE ASCENDING EARLSTON LINN
Earlston Linn was a casualty of the Galloway Hydro-Electric Scheme. On his visit there when he was preparing his *Highways and Byways in Galloway and Carrick,* published in 1916, the Revd C H Dick saw a large grilse leap out of the pool and fall into the cascade about a third of the way up. *During the next two hours a fish rose and attempted the ascent every few minutes. The proportion of misdirected leaps was fairly large. A fish would strike its whole side against a rock with a sickening whack that was heard above the roar of the fall.* He recommended that visitors should obtain a permit from the Earlston factor if they wished to view the Linn from the east bank, noting that *there is no law of trespass in Scotland, but a permit obviates attempts at obstruction on the part of servants.*

BOATING ON LOCH KEN

Loch Ken is now zoned for water sports, which include sailing, motor-boating and water-skiing. There are two RSPB bird sanctuaries and it is also a favourite water for anglers. The loch has an interesting history. The smaller of the two islands in the northern half of the loch – Burned Island – was once a Baliol stronghold, commanding the Glenkens valley and the road to Ayrshire. It was held by Edward Baliol, son of John, King of Scots 1292-6, grandson of Dervorgilla, and himself claimant to the Scottish throne, until 1354 when he granted it together with other properties to William de Aldeborough and removed to Buittle. In 1356 he withdrew his claim, handing his golden crown to Edward III in return for a pension. In still earlier years it may have been the site of a crannog. The island was partly submerged when Loch Ken levels were raised by the Hydro-Electric Scheme.

CHAUFFEURS AND VEHICLES AT GARROCH BEFORE 1914
On the left Iain McCreadie stands by a Darracq; on the right William Begg's charge is probably a Clarkson.

NEW GALLOWAY CURLERS

New Galloway curlers, about 1960. From left to right: Andy Hope (the local policeman), William Gebbie (kneeling), Ewart Muir, Charlie Murray, Alec Bell, Tom Dixon, Willie Waugh, a gentleman and lady who lived at Meadowcroft, Davy Bell senior, Davy Bell junior, Douglas Wilson. The curling field was along the Newton Stewart Road. Warmer winters in the following years put an end to curling in New Galloway - but who knows what the future holds?